M000284851

MISTER ROGERS' NEIGHBORHOOD®

A JOURNAL

RP STUDIO
PHILADELPHIA

Copyright © 2019 The Fred Rogers Company

Hachette Book Group supports the right to free expression and the value of copyright. The purpose of copyright is to encourage writers and artists to produce the creative works that enrich our culture.

The scanning, uploading, and distribution of this book without permission is a theft of the author's intellectual property. If you would like permission to use material from the book (other than for review purposes), please contact permissions@hbgusa.com. Thank you for your support of the author's rights.

RP Studio
Hachette Book Group
1290 Avenue of the Americas, New York, NY 10104
www.runningpress.com
@Running_Press

Printed in China

First Edition: October 2019

Published by RP Studio, an imprint of Perseus Books, LLC, a subsidiary of Hachette Book Group, Inc. The RP Studio name and logo is a trademark of the Hachette Book Group.

The publisher is not responsible for websites (or their content) that are not owned by the publisher.

Design by Rachel Peckman

Photos on pages 23 and 43 by Walt Seng.
Photos on pages 52-53 by Richard Kelly.

ISBNs: 978-0-7624-6702-0

1010

10 9 8 7 6 5 4 3 2 1

It's a beautiful day
in this neighborhood

You make each day a special day by
just your being you.

There's only one person in the
whole world *like you*.

To love someone is to strive to accept
that person exactly the way he or she is,
right here and now.

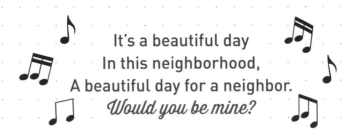

It's a beautiful day
In this neighborhood,
A beautiful day for a neighbor.
Would you be mine?

Neighbors are people who are close to us and
close to our hearts.

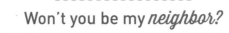
Won't you be my *neighbor?*

Things like friendship and love don't cost any
money at all, and they're very, *very* important.

We're much more than one thing.
We're much more than our arms or our legs
or our eyes or our skin or our hair. We're even
more than our thoughts. When you put us
all together, we're a beautiful, marvelous,
spirited, lovely, wonderful *one of a kind*.

Everyone has lots of ways of feeling. And all those ways of feeling are fine. It's *what we do with our feelings* that matter in this life.

As you grow, you'll find many
ways to *show people your love.*

Did you know when you marvel
you're learning?
About all kinds of wonderful,
All kinds of marvelous,
Marvelously wonderful things?

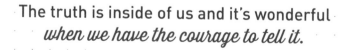

The truth is inside of us and it's wonderful *when we have the courage to tell it.*

It's important to learn to *play*.

I like you
just the way you are.

I like to know people who use their
lives to *make music for others.*

It does give you a good feeling to know that there is something you can do to help you become the master of the mad that you feel and not have to hurt yourself or anybody else. I hope that you're finding your ways of saying how you feel, ways that don't hurt you or anybody else.

It's such a good feeling to know you're alive.
It's such a happy feeling: You're growing inside.
And when you wake up ready to say,
"I think I'll make a snappy new day."

It's not so much what we
have in life that matters.
It's what we do with what we have.

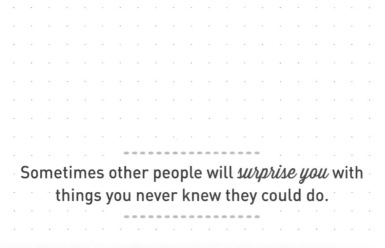

Sometimes other people will *surprise you* with things you never knew they could do.

You can grow ideas
in the garden of your mind.

Celebrate trying.

It's a good idea, don't you think?

· · · · · · · · · · · · · ·

When we think we see things that look big or
different or scary, the best thing we can do is
to be able to talk to the people we love about it.
That's what loving is all about, helping one
another feel more comfortable about who we are
and what we are seeing and hearing and thinking.
Loving is a good feeling.

· · · · · · · · · · · · · ·

You see, everybody is different, and everybody is valuable. The world can be a better place *because you were born into it.*

I hope that you'll remember
Even when you're feeling blue
That it's you I like, It's you yourself,
It's you, it's you I like.

Discovering *truth* will make me free.

I imagine you have *lots* of good ideas.

It feels good to be able to talk
about things and play about things.
It can give you a good feeling.

When you're born, you're a person.
You're not a machine. Machines just do
the same things over and over and over again.
But when you're a person,
you can grow and change and feel.

You are the only person who is exactly like
you. So in a way, you've already won in this
world because you are the only one who can be
you. The things you do are always a little
bit different than anybody else.
And that is the way it's supposed to be.

We can help each other to feel at home,
no matter where we are.

If you've got an hour,
Now's the time to share it.
If you've got a flower, wear it.
This is just the day.

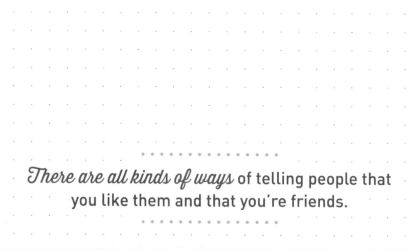

There are all kinds of ways of telling people that you like them and that you're friends.

Things don't always turn out to be just
the way we planned. But we will make
believe about that *another day*.

I feel that when I'm with people I love,
that I'm really at home.
And what a good feeling that is.

That's what learning is all about, isn't it?
A lot of it has to do with love.

You can *pretend* about things
and *dream* about things you don't
completely understand.

Whether you're first, or middle, or last,
what's important is that you're *you.*

There is something fancy about every creature in our world. And there's something fine about each one of us, too. Each person, each fish, each animal, each bird, each living creature. The important thing is to look for what's fine in everybody. And that will help us to want to take care of *everybody*.

Some people think that friends are always happy,
always having fun. Well that's not true,
friends often have hard times and sad times.
But friends can come together
again and again and build a stronger and stronger
friendship between each other.

You are my friend, you are special
You are my friend, *you're special to me.*